# ADAM-ONDI-AHMAN AND THE LAST DAYS

# ADAM-ONDI-
# AHMAN
## AND THE
# LAST DAYS

RANDALL C. BIRD

CFI
AN IMPRINT OF CEDAR FORT, INC.
SPRINGVILLE, UTAH

ISBN 978-1-59955-937-7

Published by CFI an imprint of Cedar Fort, Inc.
2373 W. 700 S., Springville, UT 84663
Distributed by Cedar Fort, Inc., www.cedarfort.com

LIBRARY OF CONGRESS CATALOGING-IN-PUBLICATION DATA

Bird, Randall C., author.
  Adam-ondi-Ahman / Randall C. Bird.
     p. cm.
  Includes bibliographical references.
  ISBN 978-1-59955-937-7
  1. Adam-Ondi-Ahman (Mo.) 2. Church of Jesus Christ of Latter-day
Saints--Missouri--History. 3. Church of Jesus Christ of Latter-day
Saints--Doctrines. 4. Mormon Church--Missouri--History. I. Title.
  BX8615.M8B57 2011
  236'.9--dc23
                          2011033545

Cover design by Angela D. Olsen
Cover design © 2011 by Lyle Mortimer
Edited and typeset by Emily S. Chambers

Printed in the United States of America

10  9  8  7  6  5  4  3  2  1

Printed on acid-free paper

# ACKNOWLEDGMENTS

A special thanks to Carla, Angela, Erika, Meisha, Rachel, Mike and Scott who encouraged me to write this book. And also thanks go to Gary B. Wells, Leland Gentry, and Robert Matthews, whose articles helped lead me to several statements used within this book's covers.

Also to Elder H. Burke Peterson for his untiring service.

# CONTENTS

# PREFACE

Recently, I read a newspaper article entitled, "2010's world gone wild: Quakes, floods, blizzards—Natural disasters killed at least a quarter million people in 2010—the deadliest year in more than a generation" (By Julie Reed Bell, Seth Borenstein of *The Associated Press*). The article went on to say that "This was the year the Earth struck back. Earthquakes, heat waves, floods, volcanoes, super typhoons, blizzards, landslides, and droughts killed at least a quarter million people in 2010—the deadliest year in more than a generation. More people were killed worldwide by natural disasters this year than have been killed in terrorism attacks in the past 40 years combined." Many of us will remember such tragic events as the volcanic activity in Iceland.

Many commercial flights were grounded for weeks waiting for this plume of ash to diminish.

Volcanic activity in Iceland

How can we ever forget those images of snow that fell upon major cities across the United States. Record snowfall cancelled flights and closed roads and schools, creating havoc for all who experienced it.

Snowfall in the U.S.

Forest and peat bog fires raced across Russia's central and western front, leaving many homeless.

Fires in Russia

Last, we will never forget the recent tragedy in Japan where an unequalled 9.0 earthquake ripped through the country and was then followed by, not only a tsunami of horrific proportions, but radiation spewing from damaged nuclear reactors.

Tsunami in Japan

We truly live in perilous times. The earth seems to be striking back. A recent chart shows that the amount of disasters in this world have increased dramatically.

Notice the increase since 1975. Prior to that time the earth maintained approximately 20-40 reported disasters a year. Even taking into account that some reporting didn't occur previously, we now approach the 450 mark yearly.

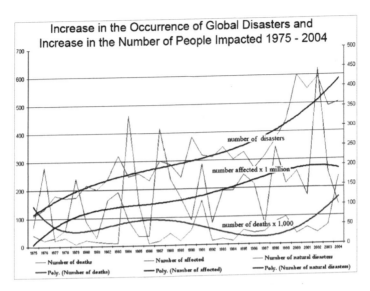

Increase in the Occurrence of Global Disasters and Increase in the Number of People Impacted 1975 - 2004

President Henry B. Eyring, in January of 2005, said,

Change is also accelerating in the world around us. Some of that change . . . is for the better. But much of the acceleration in the world is in troubles long prophesied for the last days. Each time you watch the evening news, you see stark evidence of that. You remember this scripture: "For behold, at that day shall he [meaning Satan] rage in the hearts of the children of men, and stir them up to anger against that which is good (2 Nephi 28:20)."

The Lord told us in the time of the Prophet Joseph that war would be poured out upon all nations. We see tragic fulfillment of that prophecy, bringing with it increased suffering to the innocent.

Then in prophetic-like language he said,

The giant earthquake, and the tsunamis it sent crashing into the coasts around the Indian Ocean, is just the beginning and a part of what is to come, terrible as it was. You remember the words from the Doctrine and Covenants which now seems so accurate:

"And after your testimony cometh wrath and indignation upon the people.

"For after your testimony cometh the testimony of earthquakes, that shall cause groanings in the midst of her, and men shall fall upon the ground and shall not be able to stand.

"And also cometh the testimony of the voice of thunderings, and the voice of lightnings, and the voice of tempests, and the voice of the waves of the sea heaving themselves beyond their bounds.

"And all things shall be in commotion; and surely, men's hearts shall fail them; for fear shall come upon all people (D&C 88: 88-91)." (Henry B. Eyring, Raise the Bar, BYU-I-January 25, 2005)

With all of these disasters going on around us, we can certainly still find hope and peace in the Gospel of Jesus Christ. All of these events remind us that Christ's return is near—even at the door and that our preparation is necessary for His return. The scriptures teach that "if ye are prepared ye shall not fear" (Doctrine and Covenants 38:30). One spiritual event, at which we would all love to be in attendance, will occur in the state of Missouri at a peaceful, quiet spot called Adam-ondi-Ahman. This will happen prior to Armageddon and Christ's visit to the world in general.

# INTRODUCTION

View of Adam-ondi-Ahman

Referring to the events that will occur at Adam-ondi-Ahman, Elder Bruce R. McConkie said,

> We now come to the least known and least understood thing connected with the Second Coming. It might well be termed the best-kept secret set forth in the revealed word. It is something about which the world knows nothing; it is a doctrine that has scarcely dawned on most of the Latter-day Saints themselves; and yet it is set forth in holy writ and in the teachings of the Prophet Joseph Smith with substantially the same clarity as any of the doctrines of the kingdom.[1]

Elder Neal A. Maxwell added: "Yes, there will be wrenching polarization on this planet, but also the remarkable reunion with our colleagues in Christ from the City of Enoch. Yes, nation after nation will become a house divided, but more and more unifying Houses of the Lord will grace this planet. Yes, Armageddon lies ahead—but so does Adam-ondi-Ahman!"[2]

Ever since I first visited Adam-ondi-Ahman, I have been intrigued with its history, its geography, its serenity, the Spirit that resides there, and what the future holds for this special place. The magic of this place even caught the attention of my primary-age son, who traveled with me on one occasion to this special site. As we walked upon the site known as Tower Hill, my son began running down from the hill and into the corn fields that then existed in the plains of Adam-ondi-Ahman. He had run about one-third of the way across the field when I called to him in my normal voice from the top of the hill. He heard me clearly and turned and answered. We then communicated without any voice amplification of any kind for several minutes. My son wondered how it was that this place could acoustically work such wonders. Since that occasion, he, too, has been fascinated with Adam-ondi-Ahman.

The field my son ran through

With the events previously mentioned on my mind, I began searching for a source that combined much of what had been written on Adam-ondi-Ahman and found none. This is what caused me to write this book. I have made several trips to this sacred place, interviewed former mission presidents that presided over this land, researched much of what has been written upon the subject, and have been privileged to listen to and ask questions of Elder H. Burke Peterson, who gave me a wealth of information concerning this special spot of land.

Elder Elias S. Woodruff once said in General Conference, "I sometimes wish that every member of the Church could have the privilege of going to . . . Adam-ondi-Ahman . . . for the impression that it gives them, [and] the increase in their faith. One cannot stand upon the hill overlooking the valley of Adam-ondi-Ahman without being very deeply impressed with the sacredness of the place."[3]

There is a special spirit that can be felt at Adam-ondi-Ahman

Though Christ has visited this earth often since His resurrection, I believe there are three major events that comprise the Second Coming of Jesus Christ. The first, about which this book will spend most of its time, is Christ's visit to Adam-ondi-Ahman, located in the state of Missouri. The second is His appearance on the Mount of Olives. And the last is His appearance to the world in general which is the one most people refer to as the Second Coming of Christ.

This book does not pretend to answer all questions that have arisen concerning this sacred place, but I hope you will enjoy reading my findings and then draw your own conclusions concerning this subject. I hope that you, too, will develop a special feeling for this sacred place.

# PART ONE

# Adam-ondi-Ahman: The Name and Place

# PART ONE

# Adam-ondi-Ahman: The Name and Place

## A Geographical Description of Adam-ondi-Ahman

Adam-ondi-Ahman is located in northwest Missouri, about 70 miles north of Independence, and 25 miles north of Far West, in Daviess County.

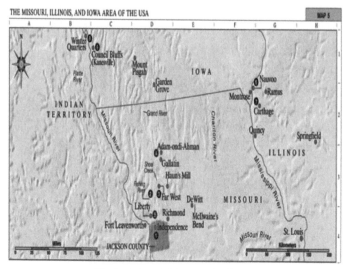

The location of Adam-ondi-Ahman
Courtesy of the Church Archives,
The Church of Jesus Christ of Latter-day Saints

The Grand River runs through the property. It was the third stake of Zion, organized on June 28, 1838 with John Smith, an uncle of the Prophet Joseph Smith, called as president. Under the order of Governor Lilburn W. Boggs, the Saints were compelled to leave Missouri in the spring of 1839, thus vacating Adam-ondi-Ahman. In 1944, Wilford C. Wood purchased thirty-eight acres at Adam-ondi-Ahman for the Church, and an additional 3,500 acres have since been purchased.

Adam-ondi-Ahman was referred to, during the Prophet Joseph Smith Jr.'s time, as Spring Hill.

"Spring Hill is named by the Lord Adam-ondi-Ahman, because, said he, it is the place where Adam shall come to visit his people, or the Ancient of Days shall sit, as spoken of by Daniel the prophet."[4] Spring Hill, located north of the valley of Adam-ondi-Ahman, is the land "through which runs the Grand River, described by the Prophet Joseph as a 'large, beautiful, deep and rapid stream, during the high waters of spring.' In the spring and summer the surrounding valley is most beautiful, with its scattered farms discernible as far as the eye can reach."[5] Adam-ondi-Ahman has also been described to be "situated on an elevated spot of ground, which renders the place as healthful as any part of the United States, and overlooking the river and the country round about, it is certainly a beautiful location."[6]

Perhaps the best description is found in a footnote in the History of the Church:

Adam-ondi-Ahman, or 'Diahman,' as it is familiarly known to the Saints, is located on the north bank of Grand River. It is situated, in fact, in a sharp bend of that stream. The river comes sweeping down from the northwest and here makes a sudden turn and runs in a meandering course to the northeast for some two or three miles, when it as suddenly makes another bend and flows again to the southeast. Grand River is a stream that has worn a deep channel for itself, and left its banks precipitous; but at 'Diahman' that is only true of the south bank. The stream as it rushes from the northwest, strikes the high prairie land which at this point contains beds of limestone, and not being able to cut its way through, it veered off to the northeast, and left that height of land standing like palisades which rise very abruptly from the stream to a height of from fifty to seventy-five feet. The summit of these bluffs is the common level of the high rolling prairie, extending off in the direction of Far West. The bluffs on the north bank recede some distance from the stream, so that the river bottom at this point widens out to a small valley. The bluffs on the north bank of the river are by no means as steep as those on the south, and are covered with a light growth of timber. A ridge runs out from the main line of the bluffs into the river bottom some two or three hundred yards, approaching the stream at the point where the bend of the river is made. The termination of the bluff is quite abrupt, and overlooks a considerable portion of the river bottom. . . . North of the ridge on which the ruins of the altar were found, and running parallel with it, is another ridge, separated from the first by a depression varying in width from fifty to a hundred yards. This small valley with the larger one through which flows Grand River, is the valley of Adam-ondi-Ahman.[7]

Aerial view of Adam-ondi-Ahman with key spots labeled

Brother Peter Lassig, the church landscaper for Temple Square, was in charge of landscaping Adam-ondi-Ahman about fifteen years ago. He said that Adam-ondi-Ahman is about the size of the University of Utah and the Brigham Young University campuses combined. He visited the site at least every six months to make sure the work was on schedule. He has not been there for several years since the landscaping was finished. However, H. Burke Peterson, who until recently was directly in charge of Adam-ondi-Ahman, along with Graham Doxey, flew back to Adam-ondi-Ahman every month to make sure everything was in readiness.

When Elder Peterson and Elder Doxey were given their assignments thirty years ago, they oversaw the work to improve and preserve the area. They planted thousands of trees, removed overgrown thorny locust trees, and performed soil renovation to keep it from washing into the Grand River. They also made roads, cut grass, built fences, and dug water ponds. Since the local farmers had planted marijuana plants for its hemp, which was greatly needed to make rope during World War II, they also found themselves removing these plants from the area.

In 2002, I had the privilege of listening to Elder H. Burke Peterson address the institute teachers at the Ogden Institute of Religion on the subject of Adam-ondi-Ahman. Following his hour long talk, we were then allowed a question and answer session with him. Four years later, on July 13, 2006, a similar event took place with the seminary and institute teachers of Utah Valley. Much of what follows is taken from notes from those two occasions.

Elder Peterson recalled that shortly after Elder Graham W. Doxey had returned from his assignment as the President of the Nauvoo Mission, President Spencer W. Kimball called him into his office and told him to begin thinking about Missouri. A short time later President Kimball called Elder Doxey back in and asked him what he had been thinking. He and Elder Peterson made, at that time, a proposal to the First Presidency that missionary couples be called to clean up the land. There was a lot of trash on the property because of the railroad that had been there. They received clearance to begin to purchase property and start the clean-up process.

In addition, the following was implemented:

- 32,000 trees planted (they had their own nursery for the first few years)

- Dwelling places for 15 couples (trailers, apartments, houses, etc.)

- 50 ponds (most man-made)

- 2 farmers to grow hay, corn, soy beans, and wheat.

- Missionaries directed to stack piles of large stones near Tower Hill, in an effort for them to be removed

Adam-ondi-Ahman has fifteen homes and two cemeteries on the property. The big cemetery was cleaned up by the boy scouts, who still keep the weeds down. The cemeteries are not a vital concern. The local people are not that interested in them, so the church simply keeps the weeds down, rather than maintain them. There is even a little pet cemetery with a dog buried there, whose name was Old Yeller. Elder Peterson was very fond of that dog.

The First Presidency has never given them a specific timeline as to when things need to be ready. They hope that members of the church will live their lives so as to always be ready for when that great day comes. Elders Doxey and Peterson alternate visits each month. They love to take their wives with them on those trips.

They report to the Prophet once or twice a year to go over budget requests and provide an accounting of the condition of the land. This meeting would take place with then President Gordon B. Hinckley. The land pays for itself with the cattle and crops that two local farmers cultivate. At the time of this talk given to CES personnel, Elder Peterson processed the missionary applications needed for Adam-ondi-Ahman. Depending on the needs of the property, anywhere from five to twelve couples were called. In the spring and summer there was more work to be done. In the fall, the staff was reduced. There have been over 200 missionary couples who have served at Adam-ondi-Ahman through the years. The work these missionaries do is described in their calls: "Those who serve here do so at the pleasure and direction of the First Presidency. On no other mission is there a shorter 'Chain of Command'. We are not proselyting missionaries. Rather, our call is as beautifiers of this sacred spot."[8] It should also be noted that at the time of writing this book, Elder H. Burke Petersen was released from his calling and succeeded by Elder Joe J. Christensen. Elder Graham W. Doxey continues to serve in his supervisory position.[9]

## Adam's Altar, Tower Hill, and Spring Hill

As the Prophet traveled through northern Missouri looking for sites to establish stakes of Zion and provide for the welfare of the Saints, the following journal entry is found dated 19 May 1838:

> This morning we struck our tents and formed a line of march, crossing Grand River at the mouth of Honey Creek and Nelson's Ferry. . . . We pursued our course up the river, mostly through timber, for about eighteen miles, when we arrived at Colonel Lyman Wight's home. He lives at the foot of Tower Hill (a name I gave the place in consequence of the remains of an old Nephite altar or tower that stood there), where we camped for the Sabbath.[10]

Tower Hill (believed site of Nephite altar)
Photo courtesy of Jeff and Marge Clayton

This comment by the Prophet Joseph, left as is, has created some confusion and controversy among members of the Church. It would have been nice if the Prophet told us more

13

about this "Nephite altar or tower." Was it really a Nephite altar? Or was it the altar Adam built as others have contended Joseph told them? Is it possible there really were two altars? But if so, why does Joseph only mention one while the people say he spoke of another?

Perhaps the easiest and most logical answer would be to assert that there were two altars. However, there are those who would disagree with that. The author expresses thanks to the work gathered by Leland Gentry in his dissertation on the subject; much of what follows is a result of his efforts.

There are basically two hills separated by a small valley that encompasses what we call Adam-ondi-Ahman. Tower Hill is one of those and is where the Prophet Joseph located the "Nephite altar."

Elder B.H. Roberts offers this information: "North of the ridge on which the ruins of the [Nephite] altar were found, and running parallel with it, is another ridge, separated from the first by a depression varying in width from fifty to a hundred yards. This small valley with the larger one through which flows the Grand River, is the valley of Adam-ondi-Ahman."[11]

Possible site of Nephite tower
Photo courtesy of Jeff and Marge Clayton

Adam built an altar on "a hill above the valley of Adam-ondi-Ahman"[12] or "plateau near Adam-ondi-Ahman [comprised of] a number of rocks piled together [where Adam] offered up sacrifices."[13]

At that place, "the Lord revealed to [Adam] the purpose of the fall and the mission of the Savior."[14]

John A. Widtsoe said that "Spring Hill [is] a hill of eminence about fifty or sixty miles north and somewhat to the east of Independence, [Missouri]"[15] and "immediately on the north side of Grand River, in Daviess county, Missouri, about twenty-five miles north of Far West."[16] It is "not far from the town of Gallatin"[17] and about one-half mile from Tower Hill. The old ruin referred to as *Tower Hill* was erroneously accepted by some as marking the site of Adam-ondi-Ahman. However, 'Tower Hill' is some half-a-mile east of that place. The tower was believed to "have some association with the first patriarch of our race, hence it has been called 'The grave of Adam.'"[18] Furthermore, Joseph Smith assigned the ruin to Nephite origin.

> [The tower] was but one of a number of such stone mounds or ruins in that vicinity: "We discovered some antiquities about one mile west of the camp [the camp was in the vicinity of Lyman Wight's house], consisting of stone mounds, apparently erected in square piles, though somewhat decayed and obliterated by the weather [erosion] of many years. These mounds were probably erected . . . to secrete treasures."[19]

It was named by Joseph Smith because of the remains of an old Nephite altar or tower that stood there. Next to Adam-ondi-Ahman was Wight's Ferry.[20]

"On May 8, 1838, Joseph Smith went to Adam-ondi-Ahman with Sydney Rigdon and Joseph Smith's clerk, George W. Robinson, 'for the purpose of selecting and laying claim to a city plat . . . called *Spring Hill*,' but by the mouth of the Lord it was named Adam-ondi-Ahman"[21] because, said the Lord, "it is the place where Adam shall come to visit his people, or the Ancient of Days shall sit, as spoken of by Daniel the prophet."[22]

High point of Spring Hill

As mentioned earlier, on "an elevated piece of ground or plateau near Adam-ondi-Ahman" was found "a number of rocks piled together . . . where [Adam] gathered his righteous posterity."[23] According to John Taylor, Joseph Smith explained that "this pile of stones was an altar built by [Adam] when he offered up sacrifices."[24] It would make sense that these stones were found in nature. Early patriarchs often erected altars to offer up sacrifices unto the Lord. These altars were not always housed in buildings, but built outside. Joseph Fielding Smith reported that "of necessity the first sanctified temples were the mountain tops and secluded places in the wilderness. If we are correctly informed, Adam built his altar on a hill above the valley of Adam-ondi-Ahman. At that place the Lord revealed to him the purpose of the fall and the mission of the Savior."[25]

Elder Heber C. Kimball recalled being with the prophet

in Daviess County, Missouri, and described the experience as follows:

> The Prophet Joseph called upon Brother Brigham, myself, and others, saying, "Brethren, come, go along with me, and I will show you something." He led us a short distance to a place where were the ruins of three altars built of stone, one above the other, and one standing a little back of the other, like unto the pulpits in the Kirtland Temple, representing the order of three grades of Priesthood; "There," said Joseph, "is the place where Adam offered up sacrifice after he was cast out of the garden." The altar stood at the highest point of the bluff. I went and examined the place several times while I remained there.[26]

When the altar was first discovered,

> It was about sixteen feet long, by nine or ten feet wide, having its greatest extent north and south. The height of the altar at each end was some two and a half feet, gradually rising higher to the center, which was between four and five feet high—the whole surface being crowning. Such was the altar at 'Diahman' when the Prophet's party visited it. Now, however, it is thrown down, and nothing but a mound of crumbling stones mixed with soil, and a few reddish boulders mark the spot which is doubtless rich in historic events.[27]

Chapman Duncan, another Church member present at these events, recalled the following:

> I think the next day, . . . he [Joseph Smith] said to these present: Hyrum Smith, Bishop Vincent [sic] Knight, myself, and two or three others, "get me a spade and I will show you the altar that Adam offered sacrifice on." I believe this was the only time Joseph was in Diamon [sic]. We went about forty rods north of my

house. He placed the shovel with care, placed his foot on it. When he took out a shovelful of dirt, it barred the stone . . . The dirt was two inches deep on the stone, I reckon. About four feet or more was disclosed. [He] did not dig to the bottom of the 3-layer of good masonry well put-up wall. The stones looked like dressed stone, nice joints, ten inches thick, 18 inches long or more. Came back down the slope perhaps 15 rods on the level. The Prophet stopped and remarked this place where we stood was the place where Adam gathered his posterity and blessed them, and predicted what should come to pass to the latest generation.[28]

Joseph Fielding Smith, Jr., stated that "When the Prophet [Joseph Smith] first visited the hill he called it 'Tower Hill, a name I gave the place in consequence of the remains of an old Nephite altar or tower that stood there,' he wrote in his journal."[29] It is unclear whether Adam's altar and that of the Nephites are different, or whether the Nephites simply used Adam's altar. As explained by Leland H. Gentry:

> The account of the discovery of 'Adam's Altar' is quite different from that for the 'Nephite altar or tower.' Abraham O. Smoot, a member of the survey team for Adam-ondi-Ahman, is quoted as having said that Joseph Smith was not present when 'Adam's Altar' was discovered: President Smoot said that he and Alanson Ripley, while surveying at the town [i.e., Adam-ondi-Ahman], which was about 22 miles from Jackson County, Missouri, came across a stone wall in the midst of a dense forest of underbrush. The wall was 30 feet long, 3 feet thick, and 4 feet high. It was laid in mortar or cement. When Joseph visited the place and examined the wall he said it was the remains of an altar built by Father Adam and upon which he offered sacrifices after he was driven from the Garden of Eden. He said that the Garden of Eden was located in Jackson County, Missouri. The

whole town of Adam-ondi-Ahman was in the midst of a thick and heavy forest of timber and the place was named in honor of Adam's altar. The Prophet explained that it was upon this altar where Adam blessed his sons and his posterity, prior to his death.[30]

Leland H. Gentry points out from his review of various descriptions that "The 'altar' was 'a quarter of a mile down the road,' rather than on top of Tower Hill where the Nephite altar was found."[31] Mr. Gentry provides a further comparison of the two altars, represented in this table:

| | Altar "A" | Altar "B" |
|---|---|---|
| Origin | Nephite or Adamic | Adamic |
| Condition | "No one stone on another in 1838 to show size or form." | Some stones scattered; but altar standing in recognizable form when having measurable dimensions. |
| Size | Stones scattered to a circle of 30 feet in diameter. | 5 or 6 feet long; another account says, "16 feet long by 9 or 10 feet wide"; 2 1/2 feet at each end but gradually rising in the center. |
| Description | Good masonry work; "dressed stone, nice joints, 10 inches thick, 18 inches or more long"; "stones of different sizes" and apparently native to the area; some partly burned and most if not all buried; first stone bared by Joseph Smith at nearly a foot deep. | Un-tooled stones but "laid accurately as any wall nowadays" in actual mortar or cement; no stones like them in the area; stones partly burned and many exposed above ground; 3 altars in rising tiers representing 3 orders of the priesthood. |
| Location | On top of the hill | "On a sidehill"; "about a quarter of a mile down the road" but also on the "highest point of the bluff" "in the midst of dense forest or underbrush"; perhaps a "tower" on the prairie. |
| Excavation | Yes | Yes |
| Approximate Discovery Date | May 18, 1838, with Joseph Smith present. | After June 20, 1838, with Joseph Smith not present.[32] |

On December 4, 1881, President John Taylor had an interview with Abraham O. Smoot about "Adam's Altar." The text of that interview follows.

John Taylor: Brother Smoot, did you see on the top of a hill, in a place called Adam-ondi-Ahman, the remains of what Joseph Smith said had been an altar built by Adam, upon which he offered sacrifice?

Abraham Smoot: Yes, sir. I first saw it in 1837, and the spring of 1838, when assisting to survey the town called by that name.

John Taylor: What was the condition of the stones of which the altar had been built?

Abraham Smoot: I remember well. The stones which lay scattered around looked as though they had been torn from a wall.

John Taylor: Yes, my remembrance is too that the stones were scattered as you say they were, having no particular form, except in one place. You remarked that you helped to make the survey; and prior to this particular conversation, you told me that you assisted in making an excavation.

Abraham Smoot: Yes, sir. I helped to excavate around the base of the altar, some 2 to 3 feet, and from 6 to 8 feet in length, which was sufficient to thoroughly satisfy us that the foundation of the wall was still there.

John Taylor: Did you examine the wall further at any later period?

Abraham Smoot: No, sir; but we intended to do so after the war, or as some called it, the "Mormon War," was over. The opportunity, however, to do so did not present itself afterwards.

John Taylor: Do you know the name of the hill where the Altar was?

Abraham Smoot: I do not recollect that. I will say that I heard Joseph say that it was the remains of an altar built by Adam; and that he offered sacrifice on it, and called his family and blessed them there.

John Taylor: That was on the point of the hill that formed a curvature?

Abraham Smoot: Yes, sir. And that point commanded a beautiful view of the country.[33]

John Taylor added:

It was stated by the Prophet Joseph Smith, in our hearing while standing on an elevated piece of ground or plateau near Adam-ondi-Ahman (Daviess Co., Missouri), where there were a number of rocks piled together, that the valley before us was the valley of Adam-ondi-Ahman; or in other words, the valley where God talked with Adam, and where he gathered his righteous posterity, as recorded in the above revelation, and that this pile of stones was an altar built by him when he offered up sacrifices, as we understand, on that occasion.[34]

Edward Stevenson, an early convert to the Church and one of the seven presidents of the Seventy, records in his journal: "I stood with Joseph Smith and others when he pointed out the sacred spot of Adam's altar. Turning to the lovely valley below us, in a large bend of Grand River, he said, 'Here is the real valley where Father Adam called his posterity together and blessed them.' He also stated that the Garden of Eden was in Jackson County—the Center Place of Zion where a great temple will be reared."[35]

Elder Alvin R. Dyer gathered reports of early brethren and residents of Daviess county which describe Adam-ondi-Ahman as the site of two ancient altars (neither of which is now to be seen) used by Adam. "One of these, an 'altar of prayer,' he locates not far from the Lyman Wight house on Tower Hill. The other, an 'altar of sacrifice,' is said to have been situated a mile or so away near the top of Spring Hill."[36] Perhaps this is the best explanation of the altars; there were actually two, not one, and they were known by different names.

Though the stones of these ancient altars have long since been dispersed, some interesting-looking structures remain at Adam-ondi-Ahman today (see accompanying picture). Several years ago while walking through this sacred site, the following structure was discovered, and a picture of the structure was submitted to a member of the Utah Archeological Association who said it was most likely an early native American altar. So it seems this sacred site of altars anciently, continued to be a similar site for the early native Americans of this country.

Possible native American altar at Adam-ondi-Ahman;
Structures of this type continue to dot the land of
Adam-ondi-Ahman today

## Moroni Stops at Adam-ondi-Ahman

The Doctrine and Covenants teaches that Moroni held
the keys to the Book of Mormon and would at some future
date partake of the sacrament with many at Adam-ondi-
Ahman.[37] Since we know that Moroni wandered these parts
of North America, I wondered if Moroni had ever visited
this sacred site of Adam-ondi-Ahman. Recently, while reading an article written by H. Donl Peterson, I found some
writings that lent support to my thoughts. Brother Peterson
states:

> Several years ago, I came across two copies of a map
> in the Archives Division of the Historical Department of
> the Church relative to Moroni's North American jour-
> neys (see Figures 1 and 2). On the back of the map in
> Figure 1 is written the following:
>
> "A chart, and description of Moroni's travels through
> this country. Got it from Br. Robert Dickson. He got it
> from Patriarch Wm. McBride at Richfield in the Sevier
> and also from Andrew M. Hamilton of same place. And
> they got it from Joseph Smith the Prophet."
>
> On the map "land Bountifull [sic]" is listed in
> "Sentral [sic] America." The cartographer wrote "start-
> ing point" below the reference to Central America.
> Above the "land Bountifull" is "Sand hills in south part
> of Arizona," and above it to the left is "Salt Lake." To
> the right is "Independens, Jackson Co, Mo." and above
> that is "Adam on Diamon, Daviess Co, Mo." To the
> right of that is "Nauvoo, Hancock C.Ill." Below that is
> "Mound Kinderhook, Pike, Co, Ill, 6 Plates Bell shape
> were found" (*were* was *was* on one copy). Then to the
> right and above that is "Kirtland, Ohio," and to the
> right of that is 'Commorre [Cumorah], N.Y.' Below this
> on the right-hand side of the map is written: "Moroni's
> Travels starting from Sentral America to the Sand hills
> Arizona then to Salt Lake U[tah], T[erritory], then to

Adam on Diammon Mo, then to Nauvoo, Ill, then to Independence Mo, then to Kirtland Ohio then to Cumoro NY."

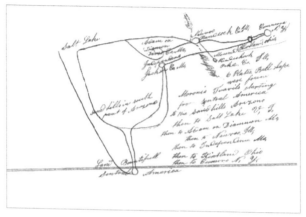

Figure 1

The second map appears to have been drawn by the same hand and is quite similar to the first, though it twice spells Arizona as Arisony (one *y* has an *a* written over it); "eden" is written near the circle identifying "Independense"; "where Adam blessed his posterity" is written near the circle identifying "Adam on Diammon"; the "missisipy river" is listed near Nauvoo; Kirtland is

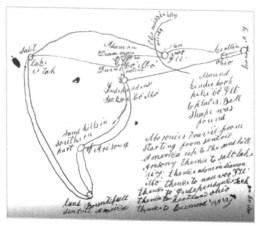

Figure 2

twice misspelled "Kertland"; and Cumorah is misspelled "Cunora" and "Cumora."

It is interesting to note that the brethren mentioned on these documents were contemporaries of the Prophet Joseph Smith, and they credited him with the notion that the travels of Moroni began in the land Bountiful, which was in Central America, and went through . . . western New York. Why Moroni took the route he did is still without answers. These men stated that the Prophet Joseph believed Bountiful is in Central America while the Hill Cumorah, the burial place of the plates, is in New York State.[38]

I certainly am not going to go into Book of Mormon geography here, but my purpose is to show that perhaps the great prophet Moroni visited this sacred site prior to his burying the plates in Cumorah.

## Relationship between Eden and Adam-ondi-Ahman

In the reading of journals one could conclude that the area of Adam-ondi-Ahman may be much more than merely that of Spring Hill and the surrounding valleys. As noted by Bruce R. McConkie:

> Far West, Missouri, also appears to be included in the land of Adam-ondi-Ahman. On April 17, 1838, the Lord commanded his saints to assemble at Far West, which place, he said, was holy ground; and there they were to build a city (D&C 115). By July 8 of that year, William Marks and Newel K. Whitney had not left their temporal concerns in Kirtland, Ohio, and were not assembling with the saints coming to Zion. In rebuking them the Lord said this: "Is there not room enough on the mountains of Adam-ondi-Ahman, and on the plains of Olaha Shinehah, or the land where Adam dwelt, that

you should covet that which is but the drop, and neglect the more weighty matters? Therefore, come up hither unto the land of my people, even Zion."[39]

Occasionally, some confusion exists as to the interrelationship between Adam-ondi-Ahman and the Garden of Eden. The Garden of Eden has sometimes been referred to as Adam-ondi-Ahman.[40]

Though there seems to be no consensus of belief among Christian scholars as to the geographical location of Eden, a majority claim that it was in Persia. We, as members of The Church of Jesus Christ of Latter-day Saints, have received revealed truth that gives us great insight concerning this matter. A revelation having been given through Joseph Smith at Spring Hill, Mo. on May 19, 1838, in which that place is named by the Lord "Adam-ondi-Ahman, because, said he, it is the place where Adam shall come to visit his people, or the Ancient of Days shall sit, as spoken of by Daniel the prophet."[41] However, they are not the same place. Adam and Eve could not have lived and raised their family in the Garden of Eden as "it was the entrance at the east of the Garden which was closed against them at the time of the 'fall.'"[42] Adam-ondi-Ahman is approximately fifty to sixty miles north and east of Independence, Missouri. The Prophet Joseph Smith has revealed that,

> The place called Independence, Jackson County, Missouri, [will be] the center place of the kingdom of God on the western hemisphere. A city called Zion or the New Jerusalem would there be built. There also, the foremost temple to the Lord should be erected. From the temple in Zion the law of the Lord would issue, as the word of the Lord would come from Jerusalem.[43]

Later, prophets close to Joseph Smith, including Brigham Young and Heber C. Kimball, have further revealed that

Independence, Missouri, is the location of the Garden of Eden.[44]

Many of the Prophet Joseph's close associates testified that the Prophet actually taught that the Garden of Eden was in or near Independence, Missouri. Heber C. Kimball, friend of the Prophet and Church leader said on one occasion: "The spot chosen for the Garden of Eden was Jackson County, in the state of Missouri, where Independence now stands; it was occupied in the morn of creation by Adam and his associates, who came with him for the express purpose of peopling this earth."[45]

Brigham Young, also a close associate of the Prophet, testified similarly that "In the beginning, after this earth was prepared for man, the Lord commenced his work upon what is now called the American continent, where the Garden of Eden was made. In the days of Noah, in the days of the floating of the ark, he took the people to another part of the earth."[46]

In conversation with Orson Hyde, on March 15, 1857, President Young said:

> You have been both to Jerusalem and Zion, and seen both. I have not seen either, for I have never been in Jackson County. Now it is a pleasant thing to think of and to know where the Garden of Eden was. Did you ever think of it? I do not think many do, for in Jackson County was the Garden of Eden. Joseph has declared this, and I am as much bound to believe that as to believe that Joseph was a prophet of God.[47]

Several years after the Prophet Joseph Smith's revelations regarding the locations of the Garden of Eden and Adam-ondi-Ahman, the *Deseret News* of September 18, 1888, published:

> A short time ago the *Washington Post* made a

remarkable statement regarding the location of the Garden of Eden. It announced that Dr. Campbell, of Versailles had lately discovered that it was on this continent, and near where St. Louis now stands. That gentleman, according to the *Post*, asserted that the Mississippi River is the Euphrates of Scripture, and that the Bible furnishes evidence of the correctness of his conclusions. It is probable that Dr. Campbell is not aware of the fact that he is not the discoverer of what he now announces, the Prophet Joseph Smith having many years ago stated that the Garden of Eden was located in what is now known as the State of Missouri. The Prophet also pointed out the precise spot where Adam offered sacrifice to the Lord, and where, as the great patriarchal head of the race, he blessed his children previous to his departure from the earth. That sacred spot in Missouri was designated by the Prophet as Adam-ondi-Ahman, the meaning of which is—the land where Adam dwelt.[48]

## The Name of Adam-ondi-Ahman

The Doctrine and Covenants states that *Ahman* is the name of God and that *Son Ahman* refers to Jesus Christ.[49] Elder Orson Pratt said:

There is one revelation that this people are not generally acquainted with. I think it has never been published, but probably it will be in the Church History. It is given in questions and answers. The first question is, "What is the name of God in the pure language?" The answer says "Ahman." "What is the name of the Son of God?" Answer, "Son Ahman—the greatest of all the parts of God excepting Ahman." "What is the name of men?" "Sons Ahman" is the answer. "What is the name of angels in the pure language?" "Anglo-man."[50]

On another occasion Elder Pratt added that the name Adam-ondi-Ahman was "The Valley of God, where Adam dwelt."[51]

More recently, Elder Alvin R. Dyer, speaking about the name said:

> The very word itself speaks of the manner in which Adam has received the *Keys of Salvation* under the counsel and direction of the Holy One, who is Jesus Christ the Lord . . . The word 'Adam' refers directly to Adam. The word 'ondi' means nearby or connected with. The word 'Ahman' means the Lord himself. Therefore a literal translation of the words 'Adam-ondi-Ahman' means 'The Lord Jesus Christ, through Adam unto mankind.'[52]

Elder McConkie stated that "Adam-ondi-Ahman, a name carried over from the pure Adamic language into English, one for which we have not been given a revealed, literal translation . . . From the early brethren who associated with the Prophet Joseph Smith, Adam-ondi-Ahman means the place or land of God where Adam dwelt."[53]

"Adam-ondi-Ahman means place or
land of God where Adam dwelt"

Other comments concerning the name Adam-ondi-Ahman range from "The valley of God in which Adam blessed his children"[54] to a public signboard signifying the site as "Adam's grave"[55] or "Adam's consecrated Land."[56]

John Taylor adds that "Adam-ondi-Ahman was referred to by the Saints as 'Di-Ahman,'"[57] while the Doctrine and Covenants revealed that "Spring Hill is named by the Lord *Adam-ondi-Ahman* because . . . it is the place where Adam shall come to visit his people, or the Ancient of Days shall sit, as spoken of by Daniel the prophet."[58]

# PART TWO

# Four Time Periods of Adam-ondi-Ahman

# PART TWO

# Four Time Periods of Adam-ondi-Ahman

Site of a sacred gathering to be held at Adam-ondi-Ahman

There are basically four major time periods when referring to Adam-ondi-Ahman. Listed below are those time periods and a brief place in scripture where you can read about them or a note about what is currently happening at the site.

1. Adam's Day—D&C 107:53-57

2. Joseph Smith's Time—D&C 78:15; 116, journals

3. Present Time—Beautify, maintain, improve the land for the Grand Council

4. Second Coming—Daniel 7; D&C 116—accounting of the priesthood

## Adam's Day

The Prophet Joseph Smith said, "The Garden of Eden was on the American continent located where the City Zion, or the New Jerusalem, will be built."[59] Upon expulsion from the Garden of Eden, Adam and Eve came to dwell at a place called Adam-ondi-Ahman.[60]

However, while "The Lord has revealed to us that Adam dwelt there towards the latter period of his probation. . . . Whether he had lived in that region of country from the earliest period of his existence on the earth, we know not."[61]

Yes, Adam and Eve dwelt in Adam-ondi-Ahman following their expulsion from the Garden, but it should be remembered that this sacred place was known and prepared from before the foundations of this earth. The Doctrine and Covenants teaches that the foundation of Adam-ondi-Ahman was established by Jesus Christ. It says, "That you may come up unto the crown prepared for you, and be made rulers over many kingdoms saith the Lord God, the Holy One of Zion, who hath established the foundations of Adam-ondi-Ahman."[62]

President Wilford Woodruff, commenting on the state of Adam and Eve after being cast out of the Garden of Eden, stated that Adam

> Went to Adam-ondi-Ahman to offer sacrifice, [upon offering the sacrifice] the angel of the Lord asked him why he did so. Adam replied that he did not know, but

the Lord had commanded him to do it. He was then told that the blood of bulls and goats, of rams and lambs should be spilt upon the altar as a type of the great and last sacrifice which should be offered up for the sins of the world. The first principle, then, ever taught to Father Adam was faith in the Messiah, who was to come in the meridian of time to lay down his life for the redemption of man.[63]

Adam-ondi-Ahman became "the land where Adam dwelt"[64] and "the valley where God talked with Adam."[65]

Adam-ondi-Ahman is where "the family of mortals had its beginning. It was there that mortal man learned to work by the sweat of his brow. It was there that the first mortal children were born to the first mortal parents. Mortal man first learned to communicate with his God in those valleys."[66]

Adam-ondi-Ahman was also "the site of the first death and murder on this earth. The blessings of the Savior's Atonement took on added significance there for the members of Adam's family. The first family relationships and associations were developed. In short, this area was truly a place of beginnings."[67]

Three years prior to his death, Adam, whose age would have been 927 years, called the sons of his lineage (in order with age listed by the side of each name:) Seth (797), Enos (692), Cainan (602), Mahalaleel (532), Jared (467), Enoch (305), and Methuselah (240), along with all his righteous posterity, together for a final blessing.

By latter-day revelation we know that this meeting, to which the Lord himself came, was for the purpose of giving patriarchal blessings to his posterity wherein he could outline what would befall the succeeding generations. It states:

> Three years previous to the death of Adam, he called Seth, Enos, Cainan, Mahalaleel, Jared, Enoch, and Methuselah, who were all high priests, with the residue

of his posterity who were righteous, into the valley of Adam-ondi-Ahman, and there bestowed upon them his last blessing.

And the Lord appeared unto them, and they rose up and blessed Adam, and called him Michael, the prince, the archangel.

And the Lord administered comfort unto Adam, and said unto him . . . "I have set thee to be at the head; a multitude of nations shall come of thee, and thou art a prince over them forever."

And Adam stood up in the midst of the congregation; and, notwithstanding he was bowed down with age, being full of the Holy Ghost, predicted whatsoever should befall his posterity unto the latest generation.

These things were all written in the Book of Enoch,[68] and are to be testified of in due time.[69]

The Prophet Joseph Smith described this incident: "I saw Adam in the valley of Adam-ondi-Ahman. He called together his children and blessed them with a patriarchal blessing. The Lord appeared in their midst, and he (Adam) blessed them all, and foretold what should befall them to the latest generation."[70]

President John Taylor also described these events:

Adam, before he left the earth, gathered his people together in the Valley of Adam-ondi-ah-man, and the curtain of eternity was unfolded before him, and he gazed upon all events pertaining to his descendants, which should transpire in every subsequent period of time, and he prophesied to them. He saw the flood and its desolating influence; he saw the introduction again of a people in the days of Noah; he saw their departure from the right path. He saw Abraham, Moses and the Prophets make their appearance and witnessed the results of their acts; he saw nations rise and fall; he saw the time when Jesus would come and restore the Gospel and when he would preach that Gospel to those who perished in the days of Noah; and in fact he saw everything that should transpire upon the earth, until the winding up scene. He was acquainted with the day in which we live and the circumstances with which we are surrounded.[71]

President Wilford Woodruff described this blessing as Adam's "great and last patriarchal blessing"[72] and explained that the "Holy Ghost rested upon Adam when he blessed his posterity in Adam-ondi-Ahman."[73] However, "All that happened at Adam-ondi-Ahman in those early days was but a type and a shadow—a similitude, if you will—of what shall happen at the same blessed place in the last days when Adam and Christ and the residue of men who are righteous assemble again in solemn worship."[74]

Joseph Fielding Smith explained further that "the Lord appeared unto them, and they rose up and blessed Adam, and called him Michael, the prince, the archangel. And the Lord administered comfort unto Adam, and said unto him: I have set thee to be at the head; a multitude of nations shall come of thee, and thou art a prince over them forever."[75]

Joseph Fielding Smith added that "Adam stood up in the midst of the congregation—and no such a gathering on any other occasion has this world ever seen—'and notwithstanding he was bowed down with age, being full of the Holy Ghost (he) predicted whatsoever should befall his posterity unto the last generation.' And all this is written in the book of Enoch, which shall be revealed in due time."[76]

Our current hymn book lists "Adam-ondi-Ahman"[77] as one of the hymns to be sung. I don't recall this beautiful hymn being sung that often, but enjoy its thought-provoking lyrics by William W. Phelps. President John Taylor reported the song was sung by the Saints about Adam-ondi-Ahman:

This earth was once a garden place,

With all her glories common,

And men did live a holy race,

And worship Jesus face to face,

In Adam-ondi-Ahman.

We read that Enoch walked with God,

Above the pow'r of mammon,

While Zion spread herself abroad,

And Saints and angels sung aloud,

In Adam-ondi-Ahman.

Her land was good and greatly blest,

Beyond all Israel's Canaan;

Her fame was known from east to west,

Her peace was great, and pure the rest

Of Adam-ondi-Ahman.

Hosannah to such days to come,

The Savior's second coming,

When all the earth in glorious bloom,

Affords the Saints a holy home,

Like Adam-ondi-Ahman.[78]

Site near overlook of the Valley of Adam-ondi-Ahman

## Joseph Smith's Time

The earliest record we have of the name *Adam-ondi-Ahman* is a revelation given to the Prophet Joseph Smith in March 1832 at Hiram, Ohio, now known as Doctrine and Covenants, Section 78 which reads: "Saith the Lord God, the Holy One of Zion, who hath established the foundations of Adam-ondi-Ahman; 'Who hath appointed Michael your prince, and established his feet, and set him upon high, and given unto him the keys of salvation under the counsel and direction of the Holy One, who is without beginning of days or end of life.'"[79]

It appears in early references to Adam-ondi-Ahman that a general area was indicated more than the specific land area we know today. Though the Prophet now knew of the name of Adam-ondi-Ahman as early as 1832, there is no record at this early date of his knowledge of a specific location.

Three years later, another reference to Adam-ondi-Ahman is given by the Prophet Joseph as the place where Adam gathered his posterity together three years prior to his death. It is interesting to note that even though this revelation, received in Kirtland, Ohio in 1835, mentions Adam's meeting with his posterity at Adam-ondi-Ahman, once again there is no specific geographical site given as to its location.

At a conference of the Church in September of 1837, Joseph Smith and Sidney Rigdon were asked to travel to Missouri, looking for places for the Saints to settle and also for where additional stakes of Zion could be established. They traveled to Far West, Missouri in November of 1837 and following their visit, Church members Oliver Cowdery, David Whitmer, Lyman Wight, and others began the process of surveying northern Missouri for possible settlement sites for the Saints. Their initial findings were reported to the Church a month later. In it they felt the area would be conducive for future settlements and stakes to be established. In a letter to Joseph Smith, Oliver Cowdery wrote: "I found a great many of the finest mill sites in the western country and made between forty and fifty locations."[80] The report was accepted by the Church in Missouri, but prior to acting on it, two members of the survey committee, Oliver Cowdery and David Whitmer, had been excommunicated from the Church. Additional work on the sites waited for the arrival of the Prophet Joseph Smith the following year. Not long after the Prophet's arrival, Joseph and others made a trip to Daviess County to establish a new stake of Zion. The following is given concerning that trip:

> Friday, May 18—I left Far West, in company with Sidney Rigdon, Thomas B. Marsh, David W. Patten, Bishop Partridge, Elias Higbee, Simeon Carter, Alanson Ripley, and many others, for the purpose of . . . laying off a stake of Zion; making locations, and laying claim to lands to facilitate the gathering of the Saints, . . . for the benefit of the poor, in upholding the Church of God. We traveled to the mouth of Honey Creek, which is a tributary of Grand river, where we camped for the night.

Saturday, May 19—This morning we struck our tents and formed a line of march, crossing the Grand River at the mouth of Honey Creek and Nelson's Ferry. . . We pursued our course up the river, mostly through timber, for about eighteen miles, when we arrived at Colonel Lyman Wight's home.[81]

Lyman Wight's second cabin in the valley of
Adam-ondi-Ahman in northwest Missouri,
a Latter-day Saint settlement from 1836 to 1838[82]

## Temple Site

A view from Spring Hill toward the Valley of Adam-ondi-Ahman;
not far from here was the temple site that was dedicated

"Not far from Spring Hill a site has been 'marked out and dedicated for a temple block.'"[83] Elder Heber C. Kimball gave further insights into this when he said,

> After hearing of the mobbing, burning and robbing in Gallatin, Daviess Co., and the region round about the brethren of Caldwell went directly to Adam-ondi-Ahman, which is on the west fork of Grand River. Thomas B. Marsh, David W. Patten, Brigham Young, myself, Parley P. Pratt, and John Taylor amongst the number. When we arrived there we found the Prophet Joseph, Hyrum Smith, and Sidney Rigdon, with hundreds of others of the Saints, preparing to defend themselves from the mob who were threatening the destruction of our people. . . . While there we laid out a city on a high elevated piece of land, and set the stakes for the four corners of a temple block, which was dedicated, Brother Brigham Young being mouth; there were from three to five hundred men present on the occasion,

under arms. This elevated spot was probably from two hundred and fifty to five hundred feet above the level of Grand River, so that one could look east, west, north or south, as far as the eye could reach; it was one of the most beautiful places I ever beheld.[84]

Thus, although "the 'temple block' was dedicated, apparently no corner stones were laid, and no temple was built."[85] The Church has since acquired the site and much of the surrounding area, which is leased to local farmers. The Adam-ondi-Ahman temple was the third temple planned but never constructed by the early Saints in Missouri. Some evidence suggests that a public square—not a temple block—was dedicated in October 1838 at Adam-ondi-Ahman. It should be noted that just prior to this event on Saturday, September 1, 1838, the First Presidency made its way from Far West to a site about halfway between Adam-ondi-Ahman and Far West—for the purpose of appointing a city of Zion. It was named the City of Seth in honor of Adam's son. The center of this city, which could have been the site of a public square and future temple, was never established due to the expulsion of the Saints from Missouri shortly after the city was appointed.[86]

Elder Alvin R. Dyer, in the company of President David O. McKay at Adam-ondi-Ahman said,

> I have been privileged to feel the nearness of President McKay's spirit. I have felt the majesty of his soul as we stood in the valley of Adam-ondi-Ahman, observing in the short distance a place there known as Spring Hill, referred to in Section 116 of the Doctrine and Covenants as the place where Adam, Michael, or the "Ancient of Days," in accordance with the prophecy of Daniel, shall in the due time of the Lord visit the earth for an important reason, and while there hearing President McKay utter quietly, "This is a most holy place."[87]

Elder Dyer, whom President McKay subsequently ordained an apostle and later set apart as a counselor in the church presidency, mentioned some interesting thoughts on the connection between Adam-ondi-Ahman and neighboring city, Far West. He said,

> In connection with President McKay's visit at Far West, it is to be noted that while there the President appeared somewhat overwhelmed. The place made a deep impression upon him; so much so that he referred to Far West a number of times in the ensuing days as a place of deep impression.
>
> The feeling that President McKay had at Far West registered upon me once again, but now with greater impact. The events that transpired there are significant: (a) The Lord proclaimed Far West a holy and consecrated land unto him, declaring to Joseph Smith that the very ground he stood on there was holy. (b) The Prophet Joseph Smith contended with the devil face to face for some time, upon the occasion of the power of evil menacing one of his children in the Prophet's home just west of the temple site. Lucifer declared that Joseph had no right to be there, that this was his place. Whereupon the Prophet rebuked Satan in the name of the Lord, and he departed and did not touch the child again. (c) The overwhelming feeling that President McKay had when he visited this sacred place.
>
> The Answer: I have often pondered the holy significance of Far West, and even more so since President McKay's visit. The sacredness of Far West, Missouri, is no doubt due to the understanding that the Prophet Joseph Smith conveyed to the brethren, at these early times, that Adam-ondi-Ahman, the place to which Adam and Eve fled when cast out of the Garden of Eden, is where Adam erected an altar unto God, and offered sacrifices, and that Far West was the spot where Cain killed Abel.

This information tends to explain why the Lord declared Far West to be a holy consecrated place; and no doubt explains why Satan claimed that place as his own, as it was here that he entered into a covenant with Cain, resulting in the death of Abel, the first of mortal existence [to die] upon this earth.

It would appear that President McKay while there felt the spirit and significance of this holy place.[88]

The beauty of Adam-ondi-Ahman and its peaceful setting allows one to be at peace while standing upon this sacred site

Just as Adam called his descendants together in the valley of Adam-ondi-Ahman to bless them, it will happen again in the timing of the Lord. The Prophet Joseph mentioned that this gathering occurred so that Adam could bless his posterity. Joseph then added that Adam "wanted to bring them into the presence of God."[89] "How did Adam bring his descendants into the presence of the Lord? The answer: Adam and his descendants entered into the priesthood order of God. Today we would say they went to the House of the Lord and received their blessings."[90] President Ezra Taft Benson, referring to this question, said:

When our Heavenly Father placed Adam and Eve on this earth, He did so with the purpose in mind of teaching them how to regain His presence. Our Father promised a Savior to redeem them from their fallen condition. He gave them the plan of salvation and told them to teach their children faith in Jesus Christ and repentance. Further, Adam and his posterity were commanded by God to be baptized, to receive the Holy Ghost, and to enter into the order of the Son of God. [See Moses 6.] To enter into the order of the Son of God is the equivalent today of entering into the fulness of the Melchizedek Priesthood, which is only received in the house of the Lord. Because Adam and Eve had complied with these requirements, God said to them, "Thou art after the order of him who was without beginning of days or end of years (Moses 6:67)."[91]

## Adam-ondi-Ahman at Present

Not too much has been written about Adam-ondi-Ahman. I'm not completely sure why, but perhaps a few members of the Church get too excited whenever they hear or read material on the subject and feel they need to pack up and move to Missouri on their own rather than wait for the priesthood to give direction. There is no visitor's center maintained there and the missionaries do not give tours to the public. At the end of his talk and time with the institute teachers, Elder H. Burke Peterson gave the following thoughts about Adam-ondi-Ahman, "I never take for granted the choice assignment I have. After 30 years of exposure to it, I still get choked up about it. This is where the ordinances of the gospel were first had by man. Adam was given the same ordinances that we have today." President Ezra Taft Benson in 1985 said that the blessings that Adam gave to his righteous posterity were the temple blessings.[92] "Adam then gave those ordinances to his family. Whenever those ordinances have been needed in other dispensations, Adam directs that work. It's a powerful thing to think that Adam and his family walked those very places. I never want to take for granted my choice assignment."[93]

## A Great Priesthood Meeting to Be Held

President Joseph Fielding Smith explained the teachings of Daniel about the great priesthood meeting to be held at Adam-ondi-Ahman:

> Daniel speaks of the coming of Christ, and that day is near at hand. There will be a great gathering in the valley of Adam-ondi-Ahman; there will be a great council held. The Ancient of Days, who is Adam, will sit. The judgment, not the final judgment, will be held where the righteous who have held keys will make their reports and deliver up their keys and ministry. Christ will come, and Adam will make his report to Him. At this council Christ will be received and acknowledged as the rightful ruler of the earth. This council in the valley of Adam-ondi-Ahman, is to be of the greatest importance to this world. At that time there will be a transfer of authority from the usurper and imposter, Lucifer, to the rightful King, Jesus Christ.[94]

Isn't it interesting to note that Lucifer will "transfer his authority" to Jesus Christ? Yes, the god of this world, even Lucifer, is set to be bound by God and the righteousness of His Saints. Though this may not happen at this exact moment, the stage is set for the winding up scenes of this earth to begin. President Smith continues,

> Judgment will be set and all who have held keys will make their reports and deliver their stewardships, as they shall be required. Adam will direct this judgment, and then he will make his report, as the one holding the keys for this earth, to his Superior Officer, Jesus Christ. Our Lord will then assume the reins of government; directions

will be given to . . . the Priesthood there assembled. This grand council of priesthood will be composed, not only of those who are faithful who now dwell on this earth, but also of the prophets and apostles of old, who have had directing authority. Others may also be there, but if so they will be there by appointment, for this is to be an official council called to attend to the most momentous matters concerning the destiny of this earth. When this gathering is held, the world will not know of it; the members of the Church at large will not know of it, yet it shall be preparatory to the coming in the clouds of glory of our Savior Jesus Christ as the Prophet Joseph Smith has said. The world cannot know of it. The Saints cannot know of it—except those who officially shall be called into this council—for it shall precede the coming of Jesus Christ as a thief in the night, unbeknown to all the world.[95]

Our Lord will then assume the reins of government; directions will be given to the Priesthood: and He, whose right it is to rule, will be installed officially by the voice of the Priesthood there assembled.

Several years ago, while attending a priesthood leadership training meeting, I had the opportunity of sitting at the feet of one of the senior members of the Quorum of the Twelve as he instructed us in our duties. During the middle of his instruction, he paused and said he would like to now allow us the opportunity to ask questions of him. I sat there pondering some questions that I had. I have always wondered, "How will you know if you are to be in attendance at the great priesthood meeting at Adam-ondi-Ahman?" As I sat there wondering if my question should be asked or if it was even appropriate, a fellow priesthood leader raised his hand and asked a question about the young adult program. This wise Apostle stared at the priesthood leader and said, "Who holds the keys in your stake?" The priesthood leader responded, "I do." Then came the firm yet loving response back from this Apostle—"Then turn them." A second question was asked by another leader with the same response back, "then turn them." We were being taught that those who hold keys of the priesthood should exercise them in behalf of those over whom they have a stewardship. I began to wonder if I should ask my question. I realized I had no keys over Adam-ondi-Ahman and so raised my hand. There was almost a sigh from the other priesthood leaders wondering why I hadn't learned from the previous two questions. I was called upon and asked my question, "How will you know if you are to be in attendance at the great priesthood meeting at Adam-ondi-Ahman?" The response that came was "Now, that was a good question." He then answered by saying, "If you are to be at Adam-ondi-Ahman, it will be a priesthood call by appointment." I felt thrilled that I had asked a good question, but then wanted to follow up my answer with, "How will the call come" or, "What do you mean a priesthood call by appointment?" I was left with an answer, but still somewhat confused as to what was taught. I probably felt much like Joseph Smith when he asked the Lord when the Second Coming would be and was told if he lived to be 85 he'd see the Lord's face. What did that mean? Yes, my question was answered, but I was left to ponder upon what it all meant. President Joseph Fielding Smith, referring to those who would attend that great meeting at Adam-ondi-Ahman said, "Others may also be there, but if so they will be there by appointment, for this is to be an official council called to attend to the most momentous matters concerning the destiny of this earth."[96]

A short time later my wife and I were traveling to Idaho and had an opportunity for a great conversation about Adam-ondi-Ahman and that great future event. It must have been dinner time, because I wondered how the hundreds of thousands and possibly more would be fed while gathered there. My wife said, "Do you remember from scripture where Christ fed thousands with a few loaves and fishes?" I certainly had to agree that with God all things are possible. But then, my questions continued. I asked, "But with that many people how would other needs be taken care of, such as restrooms?" That question went unanswered. However, this did lead us into a very enjoyable discussion sharing thoughts and insights to "priesthood call, by appointment."

What I now share is just two people having a discussion and certainly not any official doctrine of the Church, but it is interesting to look at some possibilities of how this statement could be fulfilled. My wife then said, "Do you remember when you received a letter from the First Presidency asking you to host a live broadcast of the dedication of the Nauvoo temple?" I replied, "Yes," and my wife responded with "What did the letter ask you to do?" I told her that it asked me to secure the stake center as if it were a temple. That when the broadcast began, to secure the building and not allow anyone in who didn't have a recommend from their bishop. Then she smiled and said, "Were there different times that stake members could attend?" Again, I responded "Yes." Then it suddenly came to me that this broadcast of the dedication of a temple was by appointment (each stake member was given a time to attend the dedication), and it was under the direction of the priesthood (bishops issued recommends to worthy members of the Church to attend). Could it be possible that stake members around the world, with the aid of technology that exists, could see the gathering at Adam-ondi-Ahman at their stake centers rather than be present in person for the glorious event? I don't know, and it probably doesn't really matter, except to know that some day there will be a great priesthood gathering at Adam-ondi-Ahman, and I am sure we would all like to be there. Doctrine and Covenants 27:14

indicates that all worthy members of the Church (male and female) would be in attendance. Elder Bruce R. McConkie said that "every faithful person in the whole history of the world, every person who has lived as to merit eternal life in the kingdom of the Father will be in attendance and will partake, with the Lord, of the sacrament."[97]

He further added: "The sacrament is to be administered in a future day, on this earth, when the Lord Jesus is present, and when all righteous of all ages are present. This, of course, will be a part of the grand council at Adam-ondi-Ahman."[98]

> This great council [would include] every prophet, apostle, president, bishop, elder, or church officer of whatever degree—all who have held keys shall stand before him who holds all of the keys. They will then be called upon to give an account of their stewardships and to report how and in what manner they have used their priesthood and their keys for the salvation of men within the sphere of their appointments.[99]

Some have wondered at the need to have all those who have lived on the earth prior to this great event, as well as those righteous who now live on this earth to be in attendance at this Grand Council at Adam-ondi-Ahman. Elder Orson F. Pratt commented:

> You may ask, "Why the necessity of this vast multitude from the heavens to assemble here on the earth?" It is to fulfill many prophecies besides that of Daniel; it is to fulfill prophecies that have been predicted by all holy men that understood the great events of the latter days, that the Saints who are in heaven are to come down here on the earth, and are to be organized here on the earth, and are to be united with the Saints on the earth, as one grand company, each one understanding his place. I do not think there will be any contentions or jealousies, as for instance, whether the high Priests are greater than

53

the Seventies, but all will understand their proper place and position, because their positions will be pointed out to them by the Ancient of Days, the father and prince of all, even down to those last ordained to the Priesthood. Perhaps these records will recall the positions we are all to occupy; for I believe, to the Lord was known the end from the beginning.

But why all this? Why should it be given to all to know their proper places? Why should the books be opened, and why should the fourth beast be destroyed and the body given to the burning flame? It is explained in the same connection—"I saw in the night visions, and behold one like the Son of Man came with the clouds of heaven."

To whom does this glorious personage come? He comes to the Ancient of Days. What, that personage coming in glory, majesty and dominion, with the clouds of heaven, to the Ancient of Days! What for? In order that he might receive from him the kingdom, in its order, every person standing in his proper position, everything organized after the most perfect order. The Ancient of Days delivers up the kingdom, thus completed, to the Son of Man, whose dominion becomes so great that all peoples, nations and languages serve him; and his dominion is everlasting and shall have no end.

I do not know how there could be anything more perfect for the coming of Christ than what is here recorded. It is certainly a great and grand work; and without such a work everything would be in confusion at his coming. How great and glorious will be that period when Jesus will come in the clouds of heaven! He makes this preparation beforehand, so that there may be a people ready to receive him. People of mortality, as well as immortal beings, all knowing their positions, will form the grand Council, and they will be organized ready to receive Jesus when he comes to reign as King of kings and Lord of lords upon the earth.[100]

I, like you, have often wondered how this great gathering would be kept secret. As Daniel says, "thousand thousands . . . and ten thousand times ten thousand" will be at this great meeting. How could you not know that something of great significance was occurring? I know this; that the Lord delights in those that can keep His secrets. Elder Henry B. Eyring once counseled me that how well I kept the secrets the Lord would reveal to me would determine how much more He would communicate them to me. President Marion G. Romney, commenting on the need to keep some things sacred, stated, "I don't know just how to answer people when they ask the question, 'Have you seen the Lord?' I think that the witness that I have and the witness that each of us has, and the details of how it came, are too sacred to tell. I have never told anybody some of the experiences I have had, not even my wife. I know that God lives. I not only know that he lives, but I know him."[101] And on another occasion while in a solemn assembly within the temple, President Gordon B. Hinckley asked us not to share what was said that day in those sacred confines. I believe that those in attendance at Adam-ondi-Ahman will be those that are able to keep secret those sacred events they will witness. I find it interesting to note that "the members of the Church at large" will not know of it. Certainly, the parable of the Ten Virgins comes into play at this point—five wise and five foolish. One has to begin asking himself, "What is the average sacrament meeting attendance throughout this Church?" What percentage pay a full tithing? And even how many eligible young men serve missions? Truly, if we were to achieve 50% in each of these areas (or five wise virgins), though there would still be much room for improvement, spiritual blessings would flow to these faithful individuals. However, with 50 percent wise, that still sadly shows that another 50 percent remain foolish as to things of the Spirit and would not know of the gathering at Adam-ondi-Ahman. Thus, many "members of the Church at large" would not know of it.

President John Taylor gave us a good description of what will happen at this sacred event. He said,

> A great council will then be held to adjust the affairs of the world, from the commencement, over which Father Adam will preside as head and representative of the human family. . . .

> Then they will assemble to regulate all these affairs, and all that held keys of authority to administer will then represent their earthly course. And, as this authority has been handed down from one to another in different ages, and in different dispensations, a full reckoning will have to be made by all. All who have held the keys of priesthood will then have to give an account to those from whom they received them. Those that were in the heavens have been assisting those that were upon the earth; but then, they will unite together in a general council to give an account of their stewardships, and as in the various ages men have received their power to administer from those who had previously held the keys thereof, there will be a general account.

> Those under the authorities of The Church of Jesus Christ of Latter-day Saints have to give an account of their transactions to those who direct them in the priesthood; hence the elders give an account to presidents of conferences; and . . . those presidents and the seventies give an account to the twelve apostles; the twelve to the First Presidency; and they to Joseph, from whom they, and the twelve, received their priesthood. This will include the arrangements of the last dispensation. Joseph delivers his authority to Peter, who held the keys before him, and delivered them to him; and Peter to Moses and Elias, who endowed him with this authority on

the Mount; and they to those from whom they received them. And thus the world's affairs will be regulated and put right, the restitution of all things be accomplished, and the kingdom of God be ushered in. The earth will be delivered from under the curse, resume its paradisiacal glory, and all things pertaining to its restoration be fulfilled.[102]

Could the valley below this hill possibly be the site
of the priesthood gathering at Adam-ondi-Ahman?
Photo courtesy of Jeff and Marge Clayton

President Taylor then goes on to describe conditions that will exist following this gathering as well as people who will attend. He said,

> Not only will the earth be restored, but also man; and those promises which, long ago, were the hope of the Saints, will be realized. The faithful servants of God who have lived in every age will then come forth and experience the full fruition of that joy for which they lived, and hoped, and suffered, and died. The tombs will deliver up their captives, and reunited with the spirits which once animated, vivified, cheered, and sustained them while in

this vale of tears, these bodies will be like unto Christ's glorious body. They will then rejoice in that resurrection for which they lived, while they sojourned below.

Adam, Seth, Enoch, and the faithful who lived before the flood, will possess their proper inheritance. Noah and Melchizedek will stand in their proper places. Abraham, with Isaac and Jacob, heirs with him of the same promise, will come forward at the head of innumerable multitudes, and possess that land which God gave unto them for an everlasting inheritance. The faithful on the continent of America will also stand in their proper place; but, as this will be the time of the restitution of all things, and all things will not be fully restored at once, there will be a distinction between the resurrected bodies, and those that have not been resurrected; and, as the scriptures say that flesh and blood cannot inherit the kingdom of God, neither doth corruption inherit incorruption; and although the world will enjoy just laws—an equitable administration, and universal peace and happiness prevail as the result of this righteousness; yet, there will be a peculiar habitation for the resurrected bodies. This habitation may be compared to paradise, whence man, in the beginning, was driven.[103]

### Why Would Adam Preside at This Gathering?

Yes, "all those whom my Father hath given me out of the world"[104] will be in attendance at Adam-ondi-Ahman. The whole process leading up to this meeting was outlined by Elder Bruce R. McConkie. He said,

> Adam is the foremost spirit next to the Lord Jehovah. He is the archangel, the captain of the Lord's hosts who led the armies of heaven when Lucifer rebelled; he is Michael, the mightiest of all the spirit host save only the Lord Jesus; and he came to earth as Adam, the first man. . . . The priesthood was first given to Adam. . . . He

obtained it in the Creation, before the world was formed. Priesthood is the power and authority of God. By it the worlds were made; by it the Lord's agents do everything that is needed for the salvation of men. . . . Adam held the priesthood and the keys. "He had dominion given him over every living creature [quoting Joseph Smith]" . . . Adam is first and Noah is second, among all the inhabitants of the earth, save Jesus only, where both priesthood and keys are concerned. . . . The keys have to be brought from heaven whenever the Gospel is sent. When they are revealed from heaven, it is by Adam's authority. Adam, under the direction of the Holy One, holds the keys of salvation for all men. He presides over all dispensations; all the dispensation heads and all the prophets receive direction from him; all report their labors to him. He is the chief person in the hierarchy of God, and he directs all of the affairs of the Lord on the earth. . . .

"[Joseph Smith said] all that have had the keys must stand before him in this grand council." Every prophet, Apostle, president, bishop, elder, or church officer of whatever degree—all who have held keys shall stand before him who holds all of the keys. They will then be called upon to give an account of their stewardships and to report how and in what manner they have used their priesthood and their keys for the salvation of men within the sphere of their appointments.

"Christ is the Great High Priest; Adam next."[105]

The Twelve Apostles of the Lord who were with the Lord in His ministry in Jerusalem, shall judge the whole house of Israel meaning that portion of Israel who have kept the commandments. And none else.

There will be a great hierarchy of judges in that great day, of whom Adam, under Christ will be the chief of all. Those judges will judge the righteous ones under their jurisdiction, but Christ himself, he alone, will judge the wicked. Adam, our prince will give an accounting to Christ our King. The Prince serves the King! The King always is supreme, though he honors the Prince by giving him power and dominion over his realms for an appointed season.[106]

[Adam] is the father of the human family, and presides over the spirits of all men, and all that have had [priesthood] keys must stand before him in this grand council. . . . This [grand council] may take place before some of us leave this stage of action. The Son of Man stands before him, and there is given him glory and dominion. Adam delivers up his stewardship to Christ, that which was delivered to him as holding the keys of the universe, but retains his standing as head of the human family.[107]

It appears that this gathering will not be unlike a solemn assembly held by the Church to sustain a new prophet. Elder Orson F. Pratt said,

All the various quorums and councils of the Priesthood in every dispensation that has transpired since the days of Adam until the present time will find their places, according to the callings, gifts, blessings, ordinations and keys of Priesthood which the Lord Almighty has conferred upon them in their several generations. This, then, will be one of the grandest meetings that has ever transpired upon the face of our globe. What manner of person sought you and I, my brethren and sisters, and all the people of God in the latter days to be, that we may be counted worthy to participate in the august assemblies that are to come from the eternal worlds, whose bodies have burst the tomb and come forth immortalized and eternal in their nature?[108]

If you've ever participated in a solemn assembly when a new prophet is sustained, it is a humbling, spiritual experience. To stand by priesthood quorum, and then as the entire Church, raise the right arm to the square and sustain the newly called prophet as a Prophet, Seer, and Revelator, and President of The Church of Jesus Christ of Latter-day Saints. Many have done this in person, while a great majority have opportunity to do this via the internet, television, radio, or other media present in their homes or churches. Try to envision with me what it might be like to attend a solemn assembly at Adam-ondi-Ahman, where the sacrament would be served and then as part of the business of the meeting, to be part of a solemn assembly where we raise our right arm to the square and sustain Jesus Christ as King of Kings and Lord of Lords. What a meeting to live for.

At some future date, following this great meeting, eventually "every government in the world, including the United States, will have to become part of the government of God. Then righteous rule will be established. The earth will be cleansed; the wicked will be destroyed; and the reign of peace will be ushered in."[109] Thus, as Daniel prophesied, the Saints would possess the kingdom with Christ at the head forever.[110] The only way that we can do that is to live our lives now, so that as we are tried, tested, and are given opportunities to stand up for the Kingdom of God at all cost, then and only then will He be able to trust us with it. Can you even begin to imagine what it would be like to be in attendance at this great gathering at Adam-ondi-Ahman? Elder Bruce R. McConkie, giving us insight into what happened previously when Adam called his posterity together said,

> When the full account comes to us, we suppose we shall read of the offering of sacrifices in similitude of the sacrifice of the Only Begotten; of the testimonies borne by both men and women; of great doctrinal sermons

delivered by the preachers of righteousness who then ministered among them; and of the outpouring of spiritual gifts upon the faithful then assembled. What visions they must have seen; what revelations they must have received; what feelings of rapture must have filled their bosoms as they feasted upon the things of eternity! Did Adam speak of the great latter-day gathering at Adam-ondi-Ahman, and did the faithful see with their spirit eyes what was then to be? These and a thousand other things 'are to be testified of in due time.' But this we do know: All that happened at Adam-ondi-Ahman in those early days was but a type and a shadow—a similitude, if you will—of what shall happen at the same blessed place in the last days when Adam and Christ and the residue of men who are righteous assemble again in solemn worship.[111]

The Prophet Joseph added: "Adam . . . will call his children together and hold a council with them to prepare them for the triumph of Israel which will take place gradually after the Millennium itself has been ushered in."[112]

## The Second Coming

There are three major Second Comings which comprise what the Saints and the people of the world call "The Second Coming." At Christ's ascension into heaven in the New Testament, two angels in white apparel announced to those assembled and also to all the world Christ's return when they said, "Ye men of Galilee, why stand ye gazing up into heaven? This same Jesus, which is taken up from you into heaven, shall so come in like manner as ye have seen him go into heaven."[113] The Savior will return as promised to cleanse the earth of its corruption and to reign with His covenant people for a thousand years. The righteous in all ages look forward to His return with excitement, anticipation and great joy.

Elder Bruce R. McConkie put into perspective the events of Christ's Second Coming when he said:

> Before the Lord Jesus descends openly and publicly in the clouds of glory, attended by all the hosts of heaven; before the great and dreadful day of the Lord sends terror and destruction from one end of the earth to the other; before he stands on Mount Zion, or sets his feet on Olivet, or utters his voice from an American Zion or a Jewish Jerusalem; before all flesh shall see him together; before any of his appearances, which taken together comprise the second coming of the Son of God—before all these, there is to be a secret appearance to selected members of his Church. He will come in private to his prophet and to the apostles then living. Those who have held keys and powers and authorities in all ages from Adam to the present will also be present.[114]

Daniel saw this great event when Adam will turn over the keys of the kingdom to the Son of Man. He prophesied of its happenings when he said, "and there was given him dominion, and glory, and a kingdom, that all people, nations, and languages, should serve him: his dominion is an everlasting dominion, which shall not pass away, and his kingdom that which shall not be destroyed."[115] During this great event at Adam-ondi-Ahman,

> Christ will take over the reigns of government, officially, on this earth, and "the kingdom and dominion, and the greatness of the kingdom under the whole heaven, shall be given to the people of the saints of the Most High, whose kingdom is an everlasting kingdom, and all dominions shall serve and obey him," even Jesus Christ. . . . Until this grand council is held, Satan shall hold rule in the nations of the earth; but at that time thrones are to be cast down and man's rule shall come to an end—for it is decreed that the Lord shall make an

end of all nations. (DC 87:6.) Preparation for this work is now going on. Kingdoms are already tottering, some have fallen; but eventually they shall all go the way of the earth, and he shall come whose right it is to rule. Then shall he give the government to the saints of the Most High.[116]

Some have wondered about this kingdom that God would establish and how it would function. President John Taylor taught:

> Was the kingdom that the Prophets talked about, that should be set up in the latter times, going to be a Church? Yes. And a State? Yes, it was going to be both Church and State, to rule both temporally and spiritually. It may be asked, How can we live under the dominion and laws of the United States and be subjects of another kingdom? Because the kingdom of God is higher, and its laws are so much more exalted than those of any other nation, that it is the easiest thing in life for a servant of God to keep any of their laws; and, as I have said before, this we have uniformly done.[117]

Following the events at Adam-ondi-Ahman, Christ will make His second appearance to peoples of the earth. Though we certainly have no idea of a time frame following His appearance at Adam-ondi-Ahman until this second appearance, we do know the events that will be transpiring at this coming. President Ezra Taft Benson said,

> The second appearance of the Lord will be to the Jews. To these beleaguered sons of Judah, surrounded by hostile Gentile armies, who again threaten to overrun Jerusalem, the Savior—their Messiah—will appear and set His feet on the Mount of Olives, "and it shall cleave in twain, and the earth shall tremble, and reel to and fro, and the heavens also shall shake" (D&C 45:48).

The Lord Himself will then rout the Gentile armies, decimating their forces (see Ezekiel 38, 39). Judah will be spared, no longer to be persecuted and scattered.[118]

In the midst of this turmoil at Jerusalem, Christ will appear on the Mount of Olives to save Judah from her enemies. The Doctrine and Covenants teaches us:

And the Lord shall utter his voice, and all the ends of the earth shall hear it; and the nations of the earth shall mourn, and they that have laughed shall see their folly.

And calamity shall cover the mocker, and the scorner shall be consumed; and they that have watched for iniquity shall be hewn down and cast into the fire.

And then shall the Jews look upon me and say: What are these wounds in thine hands and in thy feet?

Then shall they know that I am the Lord; for I will say unto them: These wounds are the wounds with which I was wounded in the house of my friends. I am he who was lifted up. I am Jesus that was crucified. I am the Son of God.

And then shall they weep because of their iniquities; then shall they lament because they persecuted their king.[119]

Yes, Christ will have destroyed the nations of the earth that battled against Judah. For seven years the weapons of this war left behind are buried[120] and for seven months the dead are continually buried.[121] This great event referred to as Armageddon will cause a period of silence, not unlike the Book of Mormon peoples following their destruction.[122]

Some time after all of these events, Christ will make his final (third) appearance to the world. President Ezra Taft Benson said,

The third appearance of Christ will be to the rest of the world. . . .

All nations will see Him "in the clouds of heaven, clothed with power and great glory; with all the holy angels; . . .

"And the Lord shall utter his voice, and all the ends of the earth shall hear it; and the nations of the earth shall mourn, and they that have laughed shall see their folly.

"And calamity shall cover the mocker, and the scorner shall be consumed; and they that have watched for iniquity shall be hewn down and cast into the fire." (D&C 45:44, 49–50.)

Yes, come He will![123]

Wouldn't you love to be in attendance at this glorious event?

Adam-ondi-Ahman, the place close to where it all began (The Garden of Eden), will also be the place that prepares the world for the end (the return of Jesus Christ).

# ENDNOTES

1.  Bruce R. McConkie, *The Millennial Messiah* (Salt Lake City: Deseret Book, 1982), 578–79.
2.  Neal A. Maxwell, *Even As I Am* (Salt Lake City: Deseret Book, 1982), 121.
3.  Elias S. Woodruff, in Conference Report, October 1938, 73.
4.  D&C 116:1.
5.  Joseph Fielding Smith, *The Way to Perfection* (Salt Lake City: Deseret Book, 1970), 287.
6.  Leaun G. Otten & C. Max Caldwell, *Sacred Truths of the Doctrine & Covenants, Vol. 2* (Salt Lake City: Deseret Book, 1983), 277.
7.  Joseph Smith, Jr., *History of the Church of Jesus Christ of Latter-day Saints* (Salt Lake City: Deseret News, 1948), 3:39, footnotes.
8.  Directions given in mission call to those serving in Adam-ondi-Ahman under the direction of Elder H. Burke Petersen (author's note: current calls to Adam-ondi-Ahman no longer contain these words, but tell missionaries that they will fulfill various needs at Adam-ondi-Ahman and that their work will be for good as they embark on this special assignment).

9.  Personal interview with Elder H. Burke Petersen, Ogden Institute of Religion, 2002.

10. Joseph Smith, Jr., *History of the Church of Jesus Christ of Latter-day Saints* (Salt Lake City: Deseret News, 1948), 3:34–35.

11. Ibid., 40.

12. Joseph Fielding Smith, *Doctrines of Salvation* (Salt Lake City: Bookcraft, 1956), 2:232.

13. John Taylor, *The Gospel Kingdom* (Salt Lake City: Bookcraft, 1943), 102.

14. Joseph Fielding Smith, *Doctrines of Salvation* (Salt Lake City: Bookcraft, 1956), 2:232.

15. John A. Widtsoe, *Evidences and Reconciliations* (Salt Lake City: Bookcraft, 1960), 395–96. Arranged by G. Homer Durham.

16. Joseph Smith, Jr., *History of the Church of Jesus Christ of Latter-day Saints* (Salt Lake City: Deseret News, 1948), 3:39.

17. Joseph Fielding Smith, *The Way to Perfection* (Salt Lake City: Deseret Book, 1970), 287.

18. B. H. Roberts, *A Comprehensive History of the Church*, Vol. 1 (Salt Lake City: Deseret News Press, 1930), 32:422, fn 10.

19. Joseph Smith, Jr., *History of the Church of Jesus Christ of Latter-day Saints* (Salt Lake City: Deseret News, 1948), 3:37.

20. Joseph Fielding Smith, *Teachings of the Prophet Joseph Smith* (Salt Lake City: Deseret Book, 1976), 122.

21. Ibid.

22. D&C 116:1.

23. John Taylor, *The Gospel Kingdom* (Salt Lake City: Bookcraft, 1943), 102.

24. Ibid.

25. Joseph Fielding Smith, *Doctrines of Salvation* (Salt

Lake City: Bookcraft, 1956), 2:232.

26. Orson F. Whitney, *Life of Heber C. Kimball* (Salt Lake City: Bookcraft, 1973), 209–10.

27. Joseph Smith, Jr., *History of the Church of Jesus Christ of Latter-day Saints* (Salt Lake City: Deseret News, 1948), 3:39, footnotes.

28. Leland H. Gentry, "Adam-ondi-Ahman: A Brief Historical Survey," *BYU Studies*, Vol. 13, No. 4, 571, fn 63.

29. Joseph Fielding Smith, *The Way to Perfection* (Salt Lake City: Deseret Book, 1970), 287.

30. Leland H. Gentry, "Adam-ondi-Ahman: A Brief Historical Survey," *BYU Studies*, Vol. 13, No. 4, 565.

31. Ibid., 568.

32. Ibid., 575.

33. Ibid., 567.

34. John Taylor, *Mediation and Atonement* (Salt Lake City: Deseret News, 1979), 69–70.

35. Hyrum L. Andrus and Helen Mae Andrus, *They Knew the Prophet* (Salt Lake City: Covenant Communications, 2004), 84.

36. Robert J. Matthews, "Adam-ondi-Ahman," *BYU Studies*, Vol. 13, No. 1, 31.

37. D&C 27:5.

38. H. Donl Peterson, "Moroni, the Last of the Nephite Prophets," in *Fourth Nephi Through Moroni, From Zion to Destruction*, ed. Monte S. Nyman and Charles D. Tate Jr. (Provo, UT: Religious Studies Center, Brigham Young University, 1995), 235–49.

39. Bruce R. McConkie, *Mormon Doctrine* (Salt Lake City: Bookcraft, 1966), 19.

40. James E. Talmage, *Articles of Faith* (Salt Lake City: Deseret Press, 1977), 474, fn 3.

41. D&C 116.

42. James E. Talmage, *Articles of Faith* (Salt Lake City: Deseret Press, 1977), 474, fn 3.

43. John A. Widtsoe, *Evidences and Reconciliations*, arranged by G. Homer Durham (Salt Lake City: Bookcraft, 1960), 395.

44. Ibid., 396.

45. Heber C. Kimball, in *Journal of Discourses* (Salt Lake City: Deseret Book, 1967), 10:235.

46. Brigham Young, *Discourses of Brigham Young*, compiled by John A Widtsoe (Salt Lake City: Deseret Book, 1954), 102.

47. John A. Widtsoe, *Evidences and Reconciliations*, arranged by G. Homer Durham (Salt Lake City: Bookcraft, 1960), 396.

48. Stuy, Brian H., *Collected Discourses*, Vol. 2 (Sandy, Utah: B.H.S. Publishing, 1988); Andrew Jenson, January 16, 1891, "Joseph Smith—A True Prophet," 158.

49. D&C 78:20.

50. Orson Pratt, in *Journal of Discourses* (Salt Lake City: Deseret Book, 1967), 2:342.

51. Ibid., Vol. 18:343.

52. Alvin R. Dyer, *The Lord Speaketh* (Salt Lake City: Deseret Book, 1964), 216.

53. Bruce R. McConkie, *Mormon Doctrine* (Salt Lake City: Bookcraft, 1966), 19.

54. B. H. Roberts, *A Comprehensive History of the Church* (Salt Lake City: Deseret News Press, 1930), 1:421, fn 8.

55. Robert J. Matthews, "Adam-ondi-Ahman," *BYU Studies*, Vol. 13, No. 1, 30.

56. Public Signboard by the Missouri State Historical Society on the courthouse square, Gallatin, Missouri; John Corrill, *A Brief History of the LDS*,

28; see also Gary B. Wells, "U 43 Joseph Smith, Jr.,
*History of the Church of Jesus Christ of Latter-day Saints,
Vol. 3* (Salt Lake City: Deseret News, 1948), 34–35.

57. John Taylor, *The Gospel Kingdom* (Salt Lake City:
Bookcraft, 1943), 187.

58. D&C 116:1

59. Joseph Fielding Smith, *Doctrines of Salvation*, Vol. 3
(Salt Lake City: Bookcraft, 1956), 74.

60. Ibid.

61. Orson Pratt, in *Journal of Discourses* (Salt Lake City:
Deseret Book, 1967) 16:48.

62. D&C 78:15; Joseph Smith, Jr., *History of the Church
of Jesus Christ of Latter-day Saints* (Salt Lake City:
Deseret News, 1948), 3:40.

63. Wilford Woodruff, *The Discourses of Wilford Woodruff*
(Salt Lake City: Bookcraft, 1946), 18.

64. D&C 117:8.

65. John Taylor, *The Gospel Kingdom* (Salt Lake City:
Bookcraft, 1943), 102.

66. Leaun G. Otten & C. Max Caldwell, *Sacred Truths
of the Doctrine & Covenants* (Salt Lake City: Deseret
Book, 1983), 2:278–79.

67. Ibid.

68. Referring to the Book of Enoch, Elder Orson Pratt
has said, "When we get [the Book of Enoch], I think
we shall know a great deal about the antediluvians
of whom at present we know so little" (*Journal of
Discourses*, Vol. 19, 218). In his writings, Moses
renewed the revelations and carried on the books of
earlier prophets, according to our text, which also
includes what the Prophet Joseph entitled "Extracts
from the Prophecy of Enoch." Of this, B. H.
Roberts explains: "It will be understood . . . that the
'Prophecy of Enoch' itself is found in the 'Writings

of Moses,' and that in the text above [Moses 7] we have but a few extracts of the most prominent parts of 'Enoch's Prophecy.' " What was given to the Church in 1830 was, then, not the whole book of Enoch but only "a few extracts," a mere epitome, but one composed, as we shall see, with marvelous skill; five years later the Saints were still looking forward to a fuller text: "These things were all written in the book of Enoch, and are to be testified of in due time" (D&C 107:57). The Enoch sections of the book of Moses were published in England in 1851 under the heading, "Extracts from the Prophecy of Enoch, containing also a Revelation of the Gospel unto our Father Adam, after He was driven out from the Garden of Eden" (table of contents, first edition, pages vii–viii). There are other works, usually called *pseudepigrapha,* that contain apocalyptic books of Enoch. According to latter-day revelation, some truths could be contained in the apocalyptic Enoch books. (See D&C 91.)

69. D&C 107:53–57.
70. Joseph Fielding Smith, *Teachings of the Prophet Joseph Smith* (Salt Lake City: Deseret Book, 1976), 158.
71. Leaun G. Otten & C. Max Caldwell, *Sacred Truths of the Doctrine & Covenants, Vol. 2* (Salt Lake City: Deseret Book, 1983), 279 (citing Bruce R. McConkie, *Gospel Doctrine,* 17:372).
72. Wilford Woodruff, *The Discourses of Wilford Woodruff* (Salt Lake City: Bookcraft, 1946), 65–66.
73. Ibid., 4–5.
74. Bruce R. McConkie, *The Millennial Messiah* (Salt Lake City: Deseret Book, 1982), 580.
75. Joseph Fielding Smith, *Doctrines of Salvation* (Salt Lake City: Bookcraft, 1956), 3:163.

76. Joseph Fielding Smith, *The Way to Perfection* (Salt Lake City: Deseret Book, 1970), 288–89.

77. "Adam-ondi-Ahman," *Hymns*, No. 49.

78. John Taylor, *Mediation and Atonement* (Salt Lake City: Deseret News, 1979), 70.

79. D&C 78:15–16.

80. Leland H. Gentry, "Adam-ondi-Ahman: A Brief Historical Survey," *BYU Studies*, Vol. 13, No. 4, 555, fn 6.

81. Joseph Smith, Jr., *History of the Church of Jesus Christ of Latter-day Saints* (Salt Lake City: Deseret News, 1948), 3:34–35.

82. From the "Encyclopedia of Mormonism," Vol. 1:19, *Adam-ondi-Ahman*, LaMar C. Barrett.

83. Robert J. Matthews, "Adam-ondi-Ahman," *BYU Studies*, vol. 13, No. 1, 33.

84. Orson F. Whitney, *Life of Heber C. Kimball* (Salt Lake City: Bookcraft, 1973), 208–9.

85. Robert J. Matthews, "Adam-ondi-Ahman," *BYU Studies*, vol. 13, No. 1, 34.

86. Information found at LDSChurchTemples.com/Adam-ondi-Ahman.

87. Alvin R. Dyer, in Conference Report, October 1, 1967, 41.

88. Joseph Fielding Smith, Jr., and John J. Stewart, *The Life of Joseph Fielding Smith* (Salt Lake City: Deseret Book), 340.

89. Joseph Fielding Smith, *Teachings of the Prophet Joseph Smith* (Salt Lake City: Deseret Book, 1976), 159.

90. Ezra Taft Benson, "What I Hope You Will Teach Your Children About the Temple," *Ensign*, August 1985, 9.

91. Ibid., 8.

92. Ibid., 9.

93. Ogden Institute of Religion faculty inservice meeting, 2002.

94. Joseph Fielding Smith, *The Way to Perfection* (Salt Lake City: Deseret Book, 1970), 289–91.

95. Ibid.

96. Ibid.

97. Bruce R. McConkie, *The Promised Messiah: The First Coming of Christ* (Salt Lake City: Deseret Book, 1978), 595.

98. Bruce R. McConkie, *The Millennial Messiah* (Salt Lake City: Deseret Book, 1982), 587.

99. Ibid., 582.

100. Orson Pratt, in *Journal of Discourses* (Salt Lake City: Deseret Book, 1967), 3:44.

101. Marion G. Romney, cited in F. Burton Howard, *Marion G. Romney: His Life and Faith* (Salt Lake City, Utah: Bookcraft, 1988), 222.

102. John Taylor, *The Gospel Kingdom* (Salt Lake City: Bookcraft, 1943), 217.

103. Ibid., 216–18.

104. D&C 27:14

105. Bruce R. McConkie, *The Millennial Messiah* (Salt Lake City: Deseret Book, 1982), 581–83.

106. D&C 29:12.

107. Bruce R. McConkie, *The Millennial Messiah* (Salt Lake City: Deseret Book, 1982), 582.

108. Orson Pratt, in *Journal of Discourses* (Salt Lake City: Deseret Book Company, 1967), 17:187–88.

109. Joseph Fielding Smith, *Doctrines of Salvation*, (Salt Lake City: Bookcraft, 1956), 3:13–14.

110. Daniel 7:18, 22, 27.

111. Bruce R. McConkie, *The Millennial Messiah* (Salt Lake City: Deseret Book, 1982), 580.

112. Joseph Fielding Smith, *Teachings of the Prophet Joseph*

*Smith* (Salt Lake City: Deseret Book, 1976), 157.

113. Acts 1:11.

114. Bruce R. McConkie, *The Millennial Messiah* (Salt Lake City: Deseret Book, 1982), 578–79.

115. Daniel 7:14.

116. Joseph Fielding Smith, *The Way to Perfection* (Salt Lake City: Deseret Book, 1970), 289–91.

117. John Taylor, in *Journal of Discourses*, November 1, 1857 (Salt Lake City: Deseret Book, 1967), 6:24.

118. Ezra Taft Benson, "Five Marks of the Divinity of Jesus Christ," *New Era*, Dec. 1980, 49–50.

119. D&C 45:49–53.

120. Ezekiel 39:9.

121. Ezekiel 39:12–14.

122. See 3 Nephi 8–9.

123. Ezra Taft Benson, "Five Marks of the Divinity of Jesus Christ," *New Era*, Dec. 1980, 50.

# ABOUT THE AUTHOR

Randall C. Bird was born in Blackfoot, Idaho. He attended Ricks College and Brigham Young University where he graduated with his BS and MEd degrees in 1973.

For the past thirty-seven years Randall has been employed by the Church Educational System where he taught seminary, institute, and was manager of seminary curriculum. He was associate editor for the Book of Mormon for Latter-day Saint Families and Scripture Study for Latter-day Saint Families series.

Randall and his wife, Carla, are the parents of six children and have twenty-five grandchildren. He loves spending time with his family in sports, fishing, playing, studying the scriptures, and just having fun. He currently resides in Layton, Utah.

# NOTES

NOTES

# NOTES